PARENTS AS LEARNING PARTNERS

Parent Handbook: Build a Teaching-Learning Relationship with Your Child

Elaine Robbins Harris

Parents as Learning Partners

Copyright 2010

TABLE OF CONTENTS

CHAPTER 1: Roles and Responsibilities of Learning Partners..Page 3

CHAPTER 2: Developing the Achievement Attitude ....Page 13

CHAPTER 3: Good Habits Lead to Positive Outcomes...Page 51

CHAPTER 4: Critical Thinking Skills...............Page 73

INTRODUCTION

Parents as Learning Partners provides parents with strategies to help children develop and apply the attitude, habits and critical thinking skills requiredfor continuous learning and achievement.

From elementary school through high school, college and career, learners will encounter challenges, success, mistakes, uncertainty or failure. At all levels of learning, they can develop and apply the attitude, habits and critical thinking skills that give them a strong foundation for continuous learning and achievement.

Research has shown that parents are a major influence in the attitudes, habits and skills that children develop. No one has a greater impact on children than parents.

Children imitate what they see parents doing. They pick up on your attitude about learning and trying new challenges. This handbook provides parents with guidelines, suggestions and strategies that are designed to help children develop attitudes and habits that prepare them to be resilient as they develop a solid foundation to become lifelong learners

Being a Learning Partner does not require that a parent be an expert in Math or Science. It does require a commitment to engaging in and modeling the attitude, habits and critical thinking skills that support continuous learning and achievement.

This workbook contains a lot of suggestions for discussions and activities you will use with your children. To ensure that you help children develop the attitude, habits and critical thinking skills that lead to academic achievement, it is important that you go through the book slowly. Review the ideas, concepts and activities with children one at a time to give them an opportunity to think about what you present to them and to experiment with the suggested activities.

Try to spend 2 to 3 times a week presenting the ideas, having discussion or doing activities. Some discussions or activities may take longer than others. Be flexible and patient with yourself and your children. When you come to the end of the book, go back to the beginning and start over using the discussions and activities with new and different examples.

The attitude, habits and critical thinking skills that are presented will serve children in every learning situation they encounter as they learn and grow if you take the time to teach, model and reinforce them so they become natural actions and reactions.

To help your children develop the attitude, habits and skills that support success, you will have to make a commitment to be a learning partner.

parents who are learning partners will apply a practical step by step approach to:

- ➢ Draw from their everyday experiences to build a solid teaching/learning relationship with their children
- ➢ Commit to being a learner along with their children
- ➢ Commit to a new learning challenge and share that commitment with their children
- ➢ Share their learning experience with their children as part of the coaching experience.
- ➢ Integrate the attitude and habits into their daily routine so they become part of the family's culture

CHAPTER 1

ROLES AND RESPONSIBILITIES OF LEARNING PARTNERS

Roles and Responsibilities of Learning Partners

Learning is a continuous process. In this fast-paced, highly technological environment children must be willing and engaged participants in the learning process. We can help them to develop the attitude and the strategies that prepare them to be resilient as they manage the challenges, healthy- risk taking, successes, mistakes, uncertainty, and setbacks that are all part of learning.

When parents are Learning Partners they build teaching/learning relationships with their children by learning, modeling and reinforcing the strategies to manage the various challenges that can occur in any learning situation.

The *Parents as Learning Partners* handbook is a collection of techniques and strategies designed to enable parents to build a teaching/learning relationship with their child. Parents are provided with effective strategies to help children develop the attitudes, habits and skills that will support them in becoming lifelong learners.

Students who are successful have developed a positive attitude and specific habits that enable them to remain resilient in the face of challenge, difficulty and even failure. Once this attitude and these habits are learned they become second nature and they serve individuals well in any learning situation. We see this exhibited by a fourth grader learning fractions, a high school student working to learn a foreign language, a college student challenged by a physics assignment, a graduate student preparing for an exam for admission to an MBA program, and a new hire taking on a challenging project in a new career. In fact, if we look closely we can see this attitude and these habits exhibited at all levels of success and accomplishment. These are the habits and the attitude that enable individuals to continue to move along to higher levels of development and accomplishment. The good news is they can be learned at any time because learning is an ongoing process.

As parents, we have a wealth of knowledge and information based on our learning experiences from early childhood up to the present. Our experiences give us the opportunity to manage challenges, success, mistakes and failure. We have developed strategies that we knowingly or unknowingly apply when they are part of the learning situation. We can help our children benefit by learning from our experiences by:

- ❖ Reflecting on our own learning experience

- ❖ Identifying the lessons we learned relative to managing the challenges

- ❖ Determining how to use those lessons going forward as continuous learners

Critical thinking skills combined with good habits and a good attitude prepare children to effectively process information and solve problems. These skills are crucial for continuous learning. The development of critical thinking skills enables children to see patterns, solve problems by applying knowledge in different ways, assess situations, make judgments and present and defend opinions.

PARENTS' ROLE – SHARING WHAT YOU KNOW

EXPERIENCE IS THE BEST TEACHER. One thing we all have as adults/parents is a lot of experience. Some, probably most of these experiences will make some great stories or examples to tell your children. Even if you don't want to tell the incident exactly as it happened there is a powerful lesson to be shared. Reflect on past experiences.

WHAT WAS YOUR MOST SATISFYING LEARNING EXPERIENCE? Think about something that was very difficult at first or something you always wanted to do. This can be recent or a past experience (riding a bike, roller skating, cooking, golf, computer, swimming, tennis, completing first semester in college).

What happened?

What did you learn?

What made this learning experience so special?

Who made this learning experience so special?

What else did you learn? What did you learn about yourself?

What did you learn about learning?

Which mistakes were most helpful?

What do you know now that you didn't know before this experience?

If you were going to do it over what would you do differently?

If you were helping or teaching someone to do this, what would you tell them?

WHAT IS A LEARNING EXPERIENCE YOU WISH YOU COULD DO OVER?

What was your most challenging/difficult learning experience?

What happened?

What did you learn about yourself?

What did you learn about learning?

If you had the opportunity to do it over, what would you do differently?

Learning involves mistakes, uncertainty, doubt, risk, fear, success, failure, competition and difficulty.

What do you remember about your learning experiences?

When you think about your learning experiences do these thoughts/ideas come up?

"I got it"	"I am not good at this"	"I need help"
"It's too hard"	"I know I can do this"	"I'll keep trying"
"I will try again"	"It's no use, I can't get it"	"I will stick with this until I get it"
"I quit"	"I am going to learn how to do this"	
"I have a question"	"How should I do this?"	"I am getting better"
"I can't"	"I don't want to do this"	"I can do this"
"I don't know how"		

Do any of these sound familiar?

As you go through each of the lessons in the book you may be reminded of your own learning experience. Think about how you can use your experience to make the lesson more meaningful for your child.

This book is about getting smarter, not getting discouraged, learning from your mistakes, trying something new, working smarter, believing in yourself, thinking for yourself, and asking yourself "What can I learn here?" "How do I do this?"

This book is about developing the attitude, habits and critical thinking skills required for continuous learning and achievement. When you teach, model and reinforce the attitude, habits and critical thinking skills required for continuous learning children will begin to naturally apply them to all learning opportunities. When you are a Learning Partner and you apply the strategies presented in the book you will see:

- Children learn the habits and attitudes that help them to work hard to accomplish academic goals

- Children know that learning is challenging for everyone

- Children are willing to take a risk to learn something new

- Children are not afraid of making mistakes

- Children know they learn from their mistakes

- Children know that questions are powerful tools that help them to get smarter

- Children ask questions to gain information and get a better understanding of what they are learning

- Children know you only fail if you quit

- Children know there are things they must control if they want to succeed

- Children know that learning something new takes work and time

- Learning does not happen instantly

- Children know that helping someone else helps them to get smarter and better at what they are doing.

Children who apply the attitude, habits and critical thinking skills in this manner and bounce back when they are challenged are in THE "ACHIEVEMENT ZONE."

THE "ACHIEVEMENT ZONE" refers to the experience children have when they apply the Achievement Attitude, Smart Steps and Critical Thinking Skills to learn from their mistakes, bounce back from failure and achieve learning goals.

HOW DO WE HELP CHILDREN GET INTO THE ACHIEVEMENT ZONE?

- ❖ We help them develop a healthy attitude toward learning
- ❖ We support them in building healthy self-esteem
- ❖ We help them to develop habits and skills that enable them to manage the challenges and the successes of learning
- ❖ We teach them to learn from their mistakes
- ❖ We teach them to be "resilient learners"
- ❖ We teach them to be curious and to ask questions
- ❖ We help them to develop critical thinking skills
- ❖ We teach, model and reinforce the attitude, habits and skills that lead to continuous learning

Getting children into The Achievement Zone requires the Learning Partner to teach, model and reinforce the attitude, habits and skills that are applied naturally by resilient learners.

Smart Steps

Throughout the book there are specific actions that Learning Partners will teach, model and reinforce to children. These are the steps children will use to get into The Achievement Zone. These actions will be referred to as "Smart Steps".

Smart Step Examples:
- Correcting mistakes to learn from mistakes
- Asking for feedback to determine how to improve
- Asking for help when you need it
- Bouncing back from a failure experience
- Understanding failure is an experience not a label
- Using positive self-talk when you are successful and when you are not successful

Children are not the only ones who go into The Achievement Zone. Learning Partners, your learning experiences are great examples for your children.

Think about one of your learning experiences when you worked hard to overcome a challenge, learned from your mistakes, and did not give up despite the setbacks. This was an Achievement Zone experience.

What makes it memorable?

What were you learning?

How did you feel?

What habits helped you to achieve your learning goal?

CHAPTER 2

DEVELOPING THE ACHIEVEMENT ATTITUDE

DEVELOPING THE ACHIEVEMENT ATTITUDE

Our attitude determines what we do when it is time to take on a new or challenging task. The Achievement Attitude is important because it means you don't give up when learning something new is challenging. It is the boost that enables you to work hard to get in the Achievement Zone and stay in the Achievement Zone.

The Achievement Attitude is a mindset that is focused on improving, getting smarter and getting better. With an Achievement Attitude we are not discouraged by setbacks, failure or mistakes. With the focus on improvement and accomplishment, we bounce back and do whatever it takes to reach the goal.

- Self-esteem is defined as a person's overall evaluation of themselves. Self-esteem means you feel good about yourself and you believe in yourself. You believe that you can learn new things and keep getting better and smarter.

- Self–Esteem and the Achievement Attitude work together.

Healthy Self-Esteem Supports the Achievement Attitude:

When children have high self-esteem they are more willing to try a new task or challenge.

When children have high self-esteem they don't give up easily when a learning task is challenging.

Achievement Attitude Boosts Self-Esteem:

When children are learning and feeling a sense of accomplishment their self esteem goes up.

Self-esteem supports an Achievement Attitude and the achievement. When they try something new and succeed, self-esteem remains high.

The development of self-esteem is continuous. Parents play a big role in helping children develop healthy self-esteem.

Self-esteem is based on children's self evaluation. Parents can help them to focus on the things they do to get better and smarter.

ENCOURAGE CHILDREN:
- To feel good about their effort, their improvement and their accomplishments

PRAISE CHILDREN
- For trying something new
- For not giving up when the learning task is challenging
- For completing a task or assignment
- For helping someone who is having difficulty learning something new
- For asking for help

REMIND CHILDREN
- Not to compare themselves to others

PARENTS: Consider current situations in which you can apply the above suggestions to help build your child's self-esteem.

What are the situations?

What will you do?

What can you say to be encouraging?

Attitude is a key component in the learning process. Children's thoughts about their ability or the possible outcomes of a task have a major impact on how they approach any learning situation. Attitude has a major impact on how children react to various events that occur in the learning process. It also influences how they engage in learning.

A POSITIVE ATTITUDE INFLUENCE WHAT CHILDREN DO AND SAY.

How children feel about themselves affects everything they do… learning, goals, achievements.

SMART STEP 1:

HELP CHILDREN TO DEVELOP A POSITIVE SELF IMAGE

Teach children to use strong, colorful, positive words to describe themselves. Help them create strong, positive and powerful visions of themselves. What positive words do you use to describe your children?

_____

_____

_____

NOTES

I am...

- Alert
- Ambitious
- Organized
- Resilient
- Informed
- Neat
- Responsible
- Determined
- Motivated
- Curious
- Respectful

STRONG DESCRIPTIVE WORDS

reliable	loyal	kind	persuasive
independent	prepared	brave	ambitious
responsible	enthusiastic	resilient	curious
generous	determined	honest	obedient
thoughtful	disciplined	creative	sincere
positive	clever	friendly	optimistic
appreciative	caring	patient	helpful
trustworthy	cheerful	focused	
considerate	consistent	adventurous	
courageous	courteous	attentive	
persistent	observant	hard-working	
studious	successful		
energetic	industrious		
respectful			

SMART STEP 1 - PARENT ACTIVITIES:

- Review the sample wordlist of strong and positive words with your children.

- Ask them to pick three words that they feel describe them and tell you why they picked these words. Ask the question. What have you done to fit this description?

- How would people who know you well describe you?

SMART STEP 1 - PARENT ACTIVITIES
NEW WORDS

- Review the list and ask children to pick three words they do not know and find the definitions. Ask them if any of these words could be used to describe them.

- Ask your children, "Do you want people to use these words to describe you?"

- Ask your children, "What do you have to do to fit this description?"

- Work with your children to build the wordlist of strong, positive descriptive words by continuing to add to the list as they encounter new words in textbooks, magazines, newspapers and online.

- Review the list with your children as you add new words. Refer to the new words and use the following questions for discussion.

- Would this word describe you? Why? Why not?

Smart Step 1

CHILDREN'S ACTIVITY: WHAT ARE THE WORDS YOU WOULD USE TO DESCRIBE YOURSELF IN THESE EXAMPLES?

- You asked a friend to help you with your math assignment.

- You helped your sister with her homework.

- You made sure the little boy next door got picked for a team when the neighborhood boys were playing softball.

- You went online to get information you needed for your science project.

- You helped neighbors pick up trash thrown on the street and lawn.

- You stayed after class and asked the teacher to explain the math lesson.

- You helped the neighbors pick the weeds in their backyard after they bought you ice cream.

Developing Self-Esteem

NEVER DESCRIBE CHILDREN AS "losers" "stupid" "failure" "clumsy" "dumb"

Pride, self-respect, self-love and belief in oneself are important aspects of having a good attitude. These are crucial elements that are required to stay in the Achievement Zone.

PARENTS: Encourage children to use the word list as a resource to describe themselves and their behavior. Remind them to use strong and positive words.

SMART STEP 1- PARENT ACTIVITY –
HELP CHILDREN TO DEVELOP BELIEF IN THEMSELVES AND IN THEIR ABILITIES

Observe your children and comment on their behavior when you notice them doing positive things.

➢ Focus children's attention on effort, improvement and accomplishments so they develop a belief in themselves and their abilities.

➢ Give them opportunities to accomplish tasks that reflect their strengths and positive characteristics.

➢ Praise their effort and their strategy. Effort should be recognized and rewarded.

EXAMPLE OF PARENT COMMENTS:
"Practice is really making you better"
"I see you have your brother drilling you on your spelling words.
"I respect your determination and focus"
"Did you give your best effort?"
"I am so proud of you – you don't give up"
"What did you learn today?"

Skills and achievement come through commitment and effort. We master new concepts and learn new skills through work. As we coach children we can help them to think about learning in this manner.
<u>We must reinforce this message and model it to children</u>.

SMART STEP 2

PARENTS, ENCOURAGE CHILDREN TO USE POSITIVE SELF-TALK TO EXPLAIN THEIR SUCCESSES AND FAILURES

SELF TALK SHOULD ALWAYS BE POSITIVE TALK

Help children to be aware of how they explain to themselves the things that happen in their lives. Make sure they understand that when they talk positively to themselves they will feel good about the next task or challenge.

THOUGHTS DETERMINE ACTIONS!

How children talk to themselves about success or failure has a big impact on how they feel about themselves and on how they handle future tasks.

Model and Encourage Positive Self-Talk

When children have done well, engage in a two part conversation with them. First, encourage them to talk about what they did to accomplish a goal or to improve. Second, encourage them to talk about how they can build on that knowledge and that success to take on more challenges.

*Remind them to talk about what they can control – their effort.

WHAT DO I SAY TO MYSELF WHEN I AM DOING WELL?

SMART STEP 2 – PARENT ACTIVITIES:

GIVE EXAMPLES:

Give children examples of things you do well and things that you do not do well and how you explain these things to yourself.

Things I Do Well	My Explanation
Math	I studied with friends and asked questions.
Computer	I took a class and I practice.
Cooking	My Mom taught me. I try new recipes.

Things I Don't Do Well	My Explanation
Skating	I am afraid I might fall.
Piano	I don't practice enough.
Spanish	I stopped going to class, I don't practice.

SMART STEP 2

SMART STEP 2 – PARENT ACTIVITY 1

Talk to children about how they explain their accomplishments to themselves. Discuss these examples of statements children might use to explain their accomplishments.

➢ "I got 100% on my spelling test because I studied the words with Mom."

➢ "I got an A on my essay because I used the outline and research techniques that were taught in class. I can use the same outline and research techniques for my Social Studies paper."

➢ "My math grade improved from D to B because I asked my cousin to help me with decimals & fractions."

➢ "My science exhibit will be entered in the school science fair because I worked with my classmates and I was able to ask them to explain the things I didn't understand."

PARENTS: Talk to your children about a recent accomplishment at work or at home that took a lot of effort. Tell them what you did to achieve the accomplishment. Talk about how you would talk to yourself about this accomplishment.

SMART STEP 2 – PARENT ACTIVITY 2

Remind children that their effort enabled them to improve and accomplish a goal and they always have control over their effort. When children think they have accomplished a goal or learned a new skill because it was easy, ask them what made it easy:

Was it easy because they studied?
Was it easy because they knew the words already?
Was it easy because someone helped them?

When children perceive a task or accomplishment as easy ask them what they will have to do to make their next task just as easy.

When it is something that is not easy for you- what will you do to be successful?

"I got 100% on my spelling test because I knew these words already. I will have to study harder when I get words that are new to me or words that are more difficult."

Talking about success and outcomes in this way allows children to feel that they have control over their outcomes.

HELPING CHILDREN DEVELOP POSITIVE SELF-TALK
(When they are challenged)

NEVER ALLOW CHILDREN TO REFER TO THEMSELVES WITH NEGATIVE WORDS

Using the words "loser" "stupid" "failure" "clumsy" is not allowed. Don't describe children in that way and don't allow them to describe themselves in that way. Encourage children to take responsibility when they have not done their best or accomplished their goal.

WHAT DO I SAY TO MYSELF WHEN I AM CHALLENGED?

SMART STEP 2 – CHILDREN ACTIVITY 1

Show children your list of "Things I do well" and the explanations. Instruct children to complete the chart below.

THINGS I KNOW I DO WELL

Things I Do Well	My Explanation
1)	
2)	
3)	
4)	

If children hesitate when completing this activity, encourage them by reminding them of specific areas in which they have improved.

Examples: Writing better paragraphs, roller skating, working on the computer, solving math problems.

Encourage children to take responsibility when they have not done their best or accomplished their goal.

WHAT DO I SAY TO MYSELF WHEN I AM CHALLENGED?

ENCOURAGE CHILDREN:

- To accept responsibility: Use the power attitude and power words – "I can, I am, I will."
- To talk in terms of their effort: "This is something I will have to work Harder at to accomplish."
- To talk about what they have to do to be successful.
- To talk about what they did to accomplish other goals.

REMIND CHILDREN:

- They cannot blame the situation or someone else for their outcomes.
- There is always something they can do to manage their situation.
- They must use the word "I" and talk about what they did or will do.
- They cannot talk about what someone else did (She, He, They, You, or We is not acceptable).
- it is just as important or more important to talk positively when they are having a challenging time.
- It can be difficult for children to talk positively to themselves when things are challenging.
- If children are not successful or if they experience difficulty it is important that they understand that they have control over future outcomes.

Encourage your child to acknowledge what they did or did not do to prepare for the test or assignment AND what they can do to be better prepared in the future.

- "I missed 5 spelling words because I did not study the words. I will study each evening until I know all of the words."

- "I missed an assignment and I did not ask for make-up assignments. I will make sure that I am present and attentive in class."

- "I am having difficulty with Math. I will ask my cousin who does well in math to help me."

SMART STEP 2 ACTIVITY – CHILDREN ACTIVITY 2

Instruct children to complete the chart and indicate things they *think* they don't do well and their explanation for why they *think* they don't do well.

THINGS I DON'T THINK I DO WELL

Things I Don't Do Well	My Explanation
1)	
2)	
3)	

Have a discussion with your child about how they can explain the things they don't do well using positive words.

"What can I do about the things that I don't do well?"

TEACH CHILDREN TO TAKE CONTROL OF THEIR THOUGHTS AND THEIR LIVES

Throughout the school year (and during summer vacation) instruct children to note their successes and failures and list reasons in the chart below.

SUCCESSES	EXPLANATION
1)	
2)	
3)	

FAILURES	EXPLANATION
1)	
2)	
3)	

Encourage children to make positive statements and to take credit for their effort when they are doing well.

Remind children to speak positively about what they are doing to help them develop a positive attitude. "I have a power attitude for getting smarter and I use power words to show that I have a power attitude for getting smarter."

I AM   I CAN   I WILL

When children are struggling support them by encouraging them to use phrases similar to these examples:

EXAMPLES:

- I am reliable. When I tell my Mom I will do something for her I always do it.
- I am responsible. I can finish my homework assignments because I paid attention in class.
- I am thoughtful. I will help my little brother with his homework.
- I can finish this assignment.
- I can ask for help so I will understand my math.
- I will finish my homework before I turn on the television.

SMART STEP 2 - PARENT ACTIVITY 3: Tell a story.

Tell your children about a learning situation when you were really struggling to learn something new or challenging. Make it a fun story and tell it with excitement. Use descriptive words.

Examples:
Did you burn the first meal you cooked on your own?
Did you keep falling when you tried to stand up on your roller skates?
Did you drop the ball on your foot the first time you went bowling?
Was your Science experiment a disaster?

PARENTS TELL YOUR STORY:

PARENT & CHILD ACTIVITY: Tell your child a story about a learning situation that is challenging for you.

Ask your child to tell a story similar to the one you told, with descriptive words and make it exciting. When they finish the story, ask them what they will do next to accomplish the goal and to retell the story with the new ending.

PARENTS: Make an agreement with your children that you will continue working on your challenging situation. Tell them how you expect to work on it.

Tell them you want them to continue working on their challenging situation. Ask them how they plan to work on it. Help them with a strategy if they don't have any ideas.

BUILD A SOLID FOUNDATION

Help your children to think realistically about what happens when they are learning something new.

Effort, failure, mistakes, challenge, difficulty, commitment, resilience, feedback are all part of the learning process. When we help children to understand this we give them a foundation for life-long learning.

SMART STEP 3- JUST ASK!!!!!!!

Questions are a very important part of the learning process for children and adults. Children are often reluctant to ask questions.

- Questions help children talk comfortably with teachers, family members and adults in the community.

- Questions help children to gain additional information when they are unsure of something.

- Questions can be used as preparation for learning.

- Questions help children to build a foundation for continuous learning.

- Questions help children to take responsibility for learning.

We can help children to become comfortable asking questions.

Asking questions is an indication that you want to understand what is presented and continue learning.

1. STRESS THE IMPORTANCE OF ASKING QUESTIONS

Talk to your children about the benefits of asking questions:
- To get answers when they're confused or do not understand a lesson or assignment.
- To learn something new.
- To take responsibility for learning (How can I improve? What do I need to do to accomplish this task?).

2. ENCOURAGE CHILDREN TO BECOME COMFORTABLE ASKING QUESTIONS

(It will build their confidence!)
- Remind them that asking questions is an indication that they want to understand what is presented and continue learning.
- Give them opportunities to ask questions in various situations.
- Talk to children about community events or news events and encourage them to ask questions.
- Ask your children questions to help them recognize the benefits of questions, engage them in conversation, help with studies.

ACTIVITY: To help children get accustomed to asking questions begin with a fun activity

WHAT 5 QUESTIONS WOULD YOU ASK?

After watching a movie together, a family outing, a community event or reading a book together ask your children "what 5 questions would you ask?"

EXAMPLE: If the family has been to the zoo. The 5 questions may be questions the children would ask the lion tamer:

1. What do you feed the lions?
2. Why do they eat certain foods?
3. How do you protect yourself?
4. Do you think the lions recognize you?
5. What happens if you are late feeding the lions?

You can start by letting children ask Who, What, Where and When questions but later you want to advance to How and Why questions.

SMART STEP 4: GET CURIOUS AND GET ANSWERS

Encourage children to research topics of interest or topics that are being studied in class. We feel more comfortable asking questions when we have a knowledge base to support the questions.

CREATE OPPORTUNITIES FOR ASKING QUESTIONS
- During dinner time talk to the family about a specific event and encourage children to ask questions.
- When children have homework assignments instruct them to scan the material and identify three questions related to the topic headings. (What would you like to know?)

PARENT ACTIVITIES:
- Help children to develop the habit of asking questions in everyday discussions and in study of school subjects.
- Help children to see that questions are useful for meaningful conversation.
- Use questions to engage children in conversation during dinner.
- Explain to children that developing questions as they read will help them to go beyond gathering facts. They will develop higher levels of thought and better understand what they have read.

- Select newspaper articles that involve young people. Instruct children to read the article and write 2-3 questions that go beyond stating the facts and require thought. Instruct them to follow up by going online to seek answers to their questions.
- Discuss current events in the community with your children and ask questions that cause them to think and express their opinion. Start by asking 2 or 3 questions then instruct the children to ask 3- 4 questions.

As they become accustomed to asking questions, encourage them to reflect and provide their opinions for answers. If there are fact-based questions encourage them to go online and do research to find the answers.

EXAMPLES:
How young people are treated at a store or the shopping mall
The opening or closing of a roller skating rink
New policies that are introduced at school

Model For Your Children How You Asked Questions to Gain Knowledge and Accomplish Learning Goals

- Modeling is the best way to encourage children to adopt a specific habit.
- Parents can demonstrate to children how they learned something new by asking questions.
- Talk about your learning goals – what questions did you have to ask to work toward your goal?
- Talk about a work assignment or a new policy at work – what questions did you ask to make sure you understood?

Smart Step 5:
SET HIGH EXPECTATIONS

- ❖ Children will rise to or stoop to the expectations that you set for them.

- ❖ Constantly let your children know that you have high but realistic expectations for them.

- ❖ When communicating expectations to children, be very specific.

- ❖ Let your children know that you have high expectations and you believe they can achieve at high levels. Take the steps to support them in achieving.

COMMUNICATING HIGH EXPECTATIONS…
1. Start with clear expectations about the "Achievement Zone" at home:

- TV, music, cell-phone are off while doing homework
- Thirty minutes each evening is set aside for "correction" time

2. **Honor the expectations** you set by enforcing the guidelines, modeling the behavior and giving positive comments and praise when the expectations are met.

3. **Support children in having big dreams** for their future and encourage them to determine what is required to be an astronaut, graphic artist, or engineer.

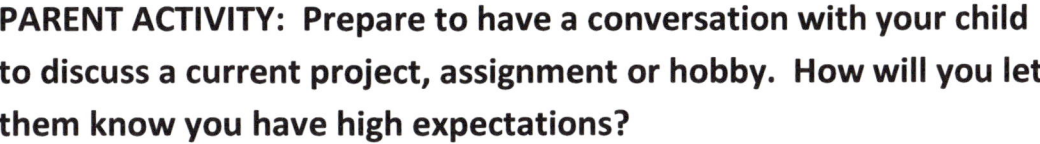

4. **Remind children to use the strategies presented in this handbook:**
- Learn from mistakes by correcting mistakes
- Set high goals and break the goal into small steps
- Learn from setbacks and failure by asking for feedback
- When you need help – ask for help

> **PARENT ACTIVITY:** Prepare to have a conversation with your child to discuss a current project, assignment or hobby. How will you let them know you have high expectations?
>
> **Be specific but realistic about what you expect**
>
> **Ask them how they will break the goal into small steps**
>
> **Be prepared to give feedback as child continues working on goal**
>
> **Support child in bouncing back from setback or failure**

SMART STEP 6 - Identify Your Success Factors

The Success Factors are the thoughts and actions we use to maintain an Achievement Attitude and stay in the Achievement Zone when learning is tough. We use our Success Factors to be resilient and "bounce back" when we are challenged or discouraged.

We all have stories about what we did to learn something new. All of the thought, preparation and actions that contributed to our success are the Success Factors.

Understanding the basics of continuous learning and achievement will help us identify our Success Factors.

LEARNING IS …
Mistakes, failure, challenges, starting over, effort and success are all part of the learning process. It is important to help children develop a positive way of thinking about every aspect of the learning process. Children can manage the learning process if they view it in a positive manner. Just like adults, children learn from their experiences.

Learning happens in small steps. You seldom learn anything after the first try. A lot of things happen when you are learning something new. Mistakes happen. Everyone makes mistakes when they are learning something new. We use the mistakes to make sure we are learning as much as we can and getting better.

Failure is sometimes part of learning. Failure only makes a bad statement about you if you quit. Failure gives you an opportunity to prove to yourself how determined and strong you are.

MISTAKES ARE….

Mistakes are a natural part of the learning process. They tell us where we need more work. They are opportunities for suggestions and learning.

What do you say when your child makes a mistake? How do you react? You should not criticize mistakes. Stress to children that we can learn from our mistakes if we take the time and effort.

"What can we learn from this?"
"What will you do next time?"
"If you had to do it over what would you do?"
"How can we correct this?"
"Errors are the only opportunity to begin again, more intelligently."
"What did you learn after you corrected your mistakes?"

PARENT ACTIVITY:

Pick one of your child's recent learning experiences. Ask him/her to write or talk about it. You have to use at least one school example but you can also use a sport or art example.

Ask some questions: What did you do to learn this? Why did you stick with it?

Tell your child to think of this as a **Learning Success Example**.

ACTIVITY: Ask your child to refer to the Learning Success Example.

What mistakes did you make while you were learning?
How did you correct them?
What did you learn?

Parents: Talk about your own Learning Success Example – answer the same questions.

WHAT IS FAILURE ANYWAY?
Failure is a natural part of learning.
Failure is an opportunity to start over.

There is a tendency to think of failure as a label or a permanent condition. It is important that we remind children that a failure is a single occurrence and they have enough control over their lives to overcome failure and be successful. It is disappointing when we don't accomplish our goals, but if it is something you really want, you can work to achieve it.

ASK CHILDREN: How can we use the experience to get smarter?

PARENTS-TELL YOUR STORY: Think of a time in your life when you experienced failure. Tell your child the story. Tell how you felt and what you did to bounce back. Did you bounce back? What did you learn? How did the experience make you smarter? Reinforce that failure is part of learning.

EFFORT…Children sometimes have a tendency to expect things to come easy. We have to reinforce the importance and benefit of effort.

This is a great time for another story. Tell a story about a time that you worked hard to achieve a goal or master something new.

What did you do to accomplish your goal?

When we ask children to consider how mistakes, failure and effort are a big part of learning anything new they can identify their Success Factors.

There are four things we want children to think about and understand whenever they are learning something new. We can use stories to focus on these four things.

> 1. Learning happens in small steps
>
> 2. Mistakes are a natural part of learning
>
> 3. Failure is a natural part of learning and is an opportunity to start over
>
> 4. Effort leads to accomplishment

Question: What were the Success Factors when you were learning how to swim or ride a bike?

_____
_____
_____

CREATE FAMILY STORIES AROUND CHILDREN'S LEARNING EXPERIENCES

Use family stories to remind children of how they have used small steps to learn new skills or new tasks. Dinner time can be story telling time.

Encourage children to tell a story of how they learned to ride a bike.

- What happened the first time they got on a bike?
- Who did the bike belong to?
- Who helped them?
- What happened when they fell off the bike?
- Why did they get back on the bike?
- What would have happened if they had not gotten back on the bike?
- Did they consider not getting back on the bike?

Encourage children to think of another learning experience they can talk about in a story. (Examples: cooking, roller skating, basketball, card game)

Encourage children to talk about an experience when they helped someone else to learn a new skill or a new task.
Examples: Riding a bike, doing a math problem, using the computer, playing a computer game

- What skill or task did they teach this person?
- How did they teach the skill or task?
- Did they person get discouraged?
- How did they prevent the person from quitting?
- What would have happened if the person had quit?
- What did they learn by teaching the other person a skill or task?
- Why is it important to help others?

Ask them to talk about a time when someone helped them to learn a new task or skill.

Ask them to talk about why it is important to ask for help.

Talk to your children about your experience helping or teaching others.
Talk about your experience when someone taught you or helped you learn a new skill or task.
These questions and the discussion they create will make great stories.

NOTES

CHAPTER 3

GOOD HABITS LEAD TO POSITIVE OUTCOMES

GOOD HABITS (Smart Steps) LEAD TO POSITIVE OUTCOMES.

We support the development of good habits by repeating simple smart steps that lead to positive outcomes.

SMART STEP 7: Learn from your mistakes by correcting your mistakes.

Errors and mistakes tell us what we don't know and what we need to focus our efforts on to get better.
Recognize that errors and mistakes are natural whenever you are learning something new. They are useful because they tell us what we don't know and what we need to focus on to get better.

> PARENT ACTIVITY: Explain to children their errors and mistakes are a natural part of learning anything new. Emphasize that Errors and Mistakes DO NOT indicate that you cannot learn something and they DO NOT indicate that you are a failure.

> CHILD ACTIVITY
> Keep a folder for all assignments and tests that are returned by teachers. Don't throw away corrected papers. Review all assignments – Set a specific time – 20 –30 minutes each evening for "correction time."

30 MINUTE-CORRECTION TIME

Review the Assignments

HISTORY, GEOGRAPHY, SCIENCE
- Go back to the book, read the section and find the correct answer.
- Write the correct answer on a sheet of paper and put it in your folder.

SPELLING: Write the correct spelling of the incorrect words.

MATH ASSIGNMENT: Ask the teacher or friend to review incorrect problems with you to determine where you made a mistake. Write the correct solution.

This is how you learn from your mistakes.

> **PARENT ACTIVITY:** At the end of the school day or after the completion of a challenging new task ask these questions:
>
> What did you learn from your mistakes today?
> What would you do differently?

DEVELOPING STRATEGIES TO STAY IN THE ACHIEVEMENT ZONE

UNCERTAINTY IS PART OF LEARNING: Sometimes we don't know what to do next – so we do whatever it takes to stay in the Achievement Zone.

SMART STEP 8) ASK FOR HELP - Sometimes we just need a little help or a simple explanation. Sometimes we may need more than a little help. It is important that we ask for whatever we need. It shows you will do whatever it takes to stay in the Achievement Zone and keep getting smarter.

SMART STEP 9) FACE YOUR FEARS: Our fears are usually exaggerated. **Use Positive Self Talk. Remember your Success Factors.** Ask yourself some questions: What are you trying to accomplish? What are your fears? What can happen if you try? What happens if you don't try? What did you do to be successful in the past? How can you use what you learned in the past?

Reflecting on past accomplishments helps to boost confidence so we can stay in the Achievement Zone.

SUGGESTIONS: Break the challenge into small steps. What can you take control of right now? How can you take control of that first step? What will you do after that first step is accomplished? Take pride in the accomplishment of each small step.

PARENTS: TELL A STORY ABOUT A RECENT SUCCESS

What was the goal? What challenges did you face? What did you have to do to be successful? What did you learn from your mistakes? How did you feel when you were having difficulty? How did you feel after you were successful? Go back to the word list – what words can you use to describe yourself after this accomplishment?

PARENTS: TELL A STORY ABOUT A CHALLENGING GOAL YOU HAVE NOT ACCOMPLISHED YET

What is the goal? What challenges are you facing now? What one thing can you do to start? What help do you need? How can you get this help? What have you done before that is similar to this goal? What did you learn from your mistakes? What questions can you ask? What words will you use to describe yourself after you have accomplished this goal?

PARENTS: Ask children to describe the goal they have been afraid of. What will they do first? Describe the goal and the first steps they will take.

_____

_____

_____

SMART STEP 10
USE POSITIVE SELF-TALK
TO MAINTAIN AN ACHIEVEMENT ATTITUDE

Always talk to yourself in strong positive language:

"I am ready for a challenge"

"I will accept the responsibility to take on this new learning challenge"

"I can do this" "I can learn this"

"I will start with one small step"

"I will not criticize myself"

"I will not compare myself to others"

"I will only compare myself to my past accomplishments"

"I will feel good about my improvement"

"When I do well in a subject or sport, I will help someone else because that helps me to improve"

PARENTS: Ask your children to tell you about a current lesson or assignment that is challenging for them. Help them develop positive self–talk about what they will do to focus on getting better.

EXAMPLE: I will show the teacher how I solved the math problem and ask her where I made a mistake.

SMART STEP 11)

"I WILL ASK FOR FEEDBACK"
(What is feedback????)
Feedback is information the teacher gives you to tell you how you are doing and what you need to do to improve

Ask for feedback or evaluation: When you are not sure how you are doing or what you can do to improve - Just ask!!!!

Ask the teacher questions to get FEEDBACK that will be helpful.

EXAMPLE: "What can I do to improve my essay writing?"

"What should I work on to improve my math skills?"

"How can I make up the work I missed?"

What part of my report should I rewrite?"

> **PARENTS:** Ask children to pick a class assignment or sport in which they want to get smarter or better. Help them think of 2 questions they can ask to get feedback so they know what to do improve.

How am I doing?

What do I need to do differently?

What are my strengths?

What do I need to work on?

Where did I make mistakes?

How can I make it better?

These are the question we have to teach children to ask themselves so they can learn from and build on each experience.

Sometimes it may be difficult to hear the answers but we cannot correct mistakes or improve if we don't have accurate information about how we are really doing.

The information we get about our progress or our achievement is called FEEDBACK.

PARENT ACTIVITY: Tell children about a recent learning activity or a new challenge at work. What questions did you ask to determine how you were doing? What did you learn from the feedback? What changes did you make? What happened after you made the changes?

Remind children it is very important to pay attention to the feedback and then make changes.
Ask children: When will you ask for feedback?

_____
_____

SMART STEP 12:
Encourage Children to Take Control When Things Get Tough

Example: "There are things in my control that can make a difference."
A feeling of control boosts confidence and willingness to take on new or challenging tasks. It is important to bounce back when things get tough.

PARENT ACTIVITY: DISCUSS CHILDREN'S ACCOMPLISHMENTS AND PROGRESS – ENCOURAGE CHILDREN TO THINK ABOUT AND TALK ABOUT WHAT THEY DID TO BE SUCCESSFUL.
Revisit assignments or tests on which they did well.

- "What did you do to get this good grade?"

- "How do you repeat this action to do well again?

PARENT ACTIVITY: WHEN THINGS ARE CHALLENGING —Ask your child these questions and have a discussion.

- What is the problem?
- What is causing you difficulty?
- What can you do about it? (There is always something you can do)
- What are the things that you can control?

PARENT ACTIVITY:
When children experience difficulty or failure, immediately direct their thinking to the things they can control.
Encourage the use of strong, positive statements to address what they can control:

I A M   I CAN   I WILL

Instruct children to name at least one thing within their control they can do when things are difficult.

PARENTS: Ask children to indicate the things over which they have control. Give them examples of the things within their control – Choosing to read the newspaper every day or going to the library are examples.

EXAMPLES:
I can pay attention.
I can study with a classmate.
I can ask for help.
I will not miss class.
I will ask questions when I don't understand or to get more information.
I will focus on what I have done to be successful in the past.
I will not compare myself to anyone else.

PARENT ACTIVITY: Sit down with your children and ask them to identify situations related to learning that are in their control.

OUT OF MY CONTROL	IN MY CONTROL
There is always a lot of activity in the house	I can find a quiet spot to do my homework
There is a spelling test every Friday	I can study spelling words every night before I watch television
I missed 3 days of school because I was sick	I can ask for help with the assignments that I missed

What are my Choices?

PARENT ACTIVITY: Talk to your children about making choices – ask specific questions.

- Did you study or did you go outside with your friends?
- Did you do your homework or did you go outside with your friends
- Did you pay attention in class or did you talk to your friends?
- Did you ask questions when you did not understand the lesson or did you sit in class feeling confused?
- Did you ask for help or did you skip the questions you did not understand?
- Did you go back and correct your mistakes or did you throw your corrected papers away?

Talk to children about the control they have in their lives. Tell them the choices they have are an opportunity to exercise that control. Discuss the consequences of each choice above.

Children learn by example.
We can teach them to make the right choices by our example.

TELL YOUR STORY:
Tell your children about a time you had to make a choice and the benefit of making the right choice.

SMART STEP 13:
ACCEPT RESPONSIBILITY - MAKE GOOD CHOICES

We always have choices.
Parents: Ask your children to talk about the results of their choices.

EXAMPLE:
- What happened because you did not pay attention in class?
- What happened because you watched television instead of studying?
- What happened when you reviewed your corrected papers and corrected the mistakes?
- What happened when you talked to your friend in class instead of paying attention?

Parents: Ask your children to talk about a choice they could have made to get better results.

Parents: Talk to children about specific events or situations. Help them to think about realistic choices.

- How do I make up the assignments I missed?
- What resources with information on this topic are available?
- What can I do to make sure my homework is done every night?
- What do I do if a friend starts talking to me in class?
- What do I do if I have to miss days in class?
- What do I do if I do not understand the lesson?
- What do I say to my friends if they are going to the park and I need to finish my homework?

PARENTS: Tell your children these are the questions to ask themselves to take make sure they take responsibility for learning.

- "What can I do to complete my assignment on time?"
- "How can I make this paper neater?"
- "What questions should I ask to get help on this assignment?"
- "What do I need to do to eliminate the distractions?"

PARENTS: Talk to your children about what it means to be responsible (for their grades and their behavior). Tell your children being responsible means being able to:

- Answer for your actions or behavior
- Choose between right and wrong

Being Responsible means - YOU DON'T BLAME OR COMPLAIN - When you are learning something new and things don't go well right away don't blame someone else or complain about the situation. Instead ask yourself some questions to determine what to do next so you don't give up.

Question must start with "What" or "How"

Question must contain the word "I" NOT the words "they" "them" "we" or "you"

Question must have an action word

EXAMPLES:

What can I do to get information for my report?

What can I do to get someone to explain the science project to me?

CREATING OPPORTUNITIES FOR SUCCESS

Success makes children feel good and encourages them to keep learning.

SMART STEP 14: TAKE SMALL STEPS TO BIG SUCCESSES – All learning challenges can be broken into small steps.

PARENTS: Point out to your children that it is a series of small steps that helps them to learn a new task or skill and each small step is an accomplishment

WE CAN CREATE OPPORTUNITIES FOR SUCCESS

- Each task or goal can be broken into "small steps"
- We can celebrate the accomplishment of each step
- Plan Small but Special Celebrations for "small step" accomplishments (special dessert, favorite meal, additional time for TV or games)
- Help children to focus on "small step" accomplishments

Develop "Small Step Success" Habits

SMART STEP 14 PARENT ACTIVITY:

1) Identify a learning goal for yourself. Select something you really want to learn.

EXAMPLES:

Learn how to use a computer   Learn a foreign language

Getting an Associates' Degree   Learn to play golf or tennis

Learn to cook new recipes   Learn to sew

Setting up a tutoring program in a church or community center

2) Share your learning goal with your children.

3) Identify the small steps that you will take to accomplish your goal.

4) Tell your children your story as you work toward accomplishing your goal.

5) Talk about your victories and your difficulties.

6) Acknowledge and celebrate each victory.

BECOME A ROLE MODEL FOR YOUR CHILDREN USING THE "SMALL STEPS" RULE.

PARENT LEARNING GOAL WORKSHEET

WHAT IS YOUR LEARNING GOAL?

_____

_____

_____

SMALL STEPS YOU WILL TAKE TO ACCOMPLISH YOUR GOAL:

_____

_____

_____

_____

CHALLENGES OR DIFFICULTIES YOU MAY ENCOUNTER:

_____

_____

_____

HOW WILL YOU MANAGE THE CHALLENGES OR DIFFICULTIES? WHAT WILL YOU DO WHEN THINGS GET TOUGH?

_____

_____

_____

WHAT SACRIFICES WILL YOU MAKE TO ACCOMPLISH YOUR GOAL?

_____

_____

_____

ENCOURAGE CHILDREN TO BREAK ALL TASKS INTO "SMALL STEPS"

Using a class or homework assignment ask your child to identify an important learning goal and break it into small steps.
Use this worksheet to prepare to take on the goal.

CHILDREN'S LEARNING GOAL- SMALL STEP WORKSHEET

1) Identify a learning goal: Think about something you have never tried before that you would like to learn:

Swimming　　　　　Skating
Sewing　　　　　　Cooking
Planting a garden　　Drama class
Learn to play a musical instrument
Learn a new computer program and teach your parents

2) Identify resources (park district, community center, library, neighbor, siblings)

3) Identify equipment and information required.

4) Break the task into small steps you will take to accomplish goal.

5) Identify difficulties or challenges you may encounter.

6) How will you manage these difficulties or challenges?

7) Determine what questions you need answered.

8) What will you do to prepare to take the first step?

PARENTS:
use these questions to discuss your goals and accomplishments with children and to support them in discussing their goals and accomplishments. After taking on a learning goal it is important to talk about the Success Factors.

Remind children that Success Factors are the thoughts and actions that contributed to your success on a particular learning goal.

What was your learning goal?

What steps did you take to start working towards your goals?

What are the thoughts and actions that contributed to your success? (These are your Success Factors)

What sacrifices did you make to get started?

What are some of the challenges you had as you worked toward your goal?

How did you manage those challenges?

What self-talk did you use when you were having difficulty?

Did you ask for help?

Who supported and encouraged you?

What choices have you had to make to continue working on your goal?

What questions did you ask?

What have you learned?

What makes you feel proud?

What is your next goal?

Smart Steps Review

PARENTS: Review the Smart Steps with children and remind them to use these strategies in every learning situation:

1. Develop a positive self image and "Achievement Attitude"
2. Use positive self-talk to explain your successes and setbacks
3. Ask questions
4. Get curious and get answers to get smarter
5. Set high expectations
6. Identify success factors - think of failure as a natural part of learning and "bounce back" when things get challenging
7. Learn from mistakes by correcting mistakes
8. Ask for help
9. Face your fears
10. Use positive self-talk to maintain "Achievement Attitude"
11. Ask for feedback
12. Take control when things get tough
13. Accept responsibility – Make good choices
14. Break a task into Small Steps

Sample statements that encourage children to use the Smart Steps:

"I know you will succeed if you break the task into small steps. You were successful when you tried that approach before."

"Failure is a natural part of learning. This is the opportunity to begin again with more information."

"Ask questions to get the information you need."

"When you go back and correct your mistakes you continue to get smarter."

CHAPTER 4

CRITICAL THINKING SKILLS

CRITICAL THINKING SKILLS

Critical Thinking Skills are:

Skills required to gather, process and use new information effectively to solve problems and generate new ideas

Skills required to effectively use current knowledge in different ways to generate new ideas and achieve new learning goals

Critical thinking is a process that requires the student to apply a number of thinking activities, in which they gather information, evaluate the information and use it effectively. The following activities contribute to critical thinking:

- Careful observation
- Remembering (recall, think back)
- Wondering (ponder, think about, puzzle over, deliberate)
- Imagining (visualize, dream, create)
- Inquiring (question, seek information)
- Interpreting (explain, define)
- Evaluating (assess, estimate, grade)
- Judging (value, size up, rank)

Critical thinking skills combined with good habits and a prepare children to effectively process information and solve problems.

Critical thinking skills are crucial for continuous learning. Development of critical thinking skills enables students to continuously apply their experiences and understanding of concepts to learning new material.

The development of critical thinking skills enables children to see patterns, solve problems by applying knowledge in different ways, assess situations, make judgments and present and defend opinions.

Development of critical thinking skills gives students a broad context to support learning and development in many situations, academic and social.

Critical thinking skills enable students to go beyond memorization and factual recall. Critical thinking involves moving beyond KNOWLEDGE (the recall of specific information) and COMPREHENSION (an understanding of what was read) to REASONING and THINKING.

Development of critical thinking skills enables students to continuously apply their understanding of concepts to learning new material.

Development of critical thinking skills gives students a broad context to support learning and development in many situations (academic and social).

Critical thinking skills are a "must" in our rapidly changing, technologically oriented world.

Effective use of questions is very important in the development of critical thinking skills.

Use questions to accomplish the following:
- Probe beyond the facts
- Identify causes
- Recognize patterns
- Judge characters
- Encourage in-depth thought and discussion
- Apply prior knowledge and skills

PARENTS: Use examples to help children think about using questions. Talk about a familiar situation at school or in the news. Use questions to help them think critically about the situation.

- **How is this situation similar to other events that have happened recently?**
- **Is there a pattern of behavior that has lead to this?**
- **What could have been done to prevent this?**
- **What can be done to address the problem now?**

USE QUESTIONS TO DEVELOP CRITICAL THINKING SKILLS

> PARENT ACTIVITY – Ask children to read an article on current events or community events or select a topic that is being debated in the community.
>
> Use the following questions to encourage children to reflect on the topic and think critically. Engage children in discussion using these questions.

Answer several of the following questions:

What are the possible outcomes of the presented situation?

What factors may have contributed to this?

What may have prevented this?

How will this impact others?

What does the author believe?

What are the inconsistencies?

What ideas justify the conclusion?

How could this have been prevented?

How does this compare to…?

What is a possible motive?

What if...?

What evidence supports the conclusion?

What is an alternative conclusion?

What are the obvious patterns?

Based on your experience and your values, how do you judge the actions or decisions of the main character of the article or story?

Developing Critical Thinking Skills

The following chapters provide the skills and strategies to help children develop the habit of thinking critically.
Several activities are involved in critical thinking:

- Careful observation
- Remembering (recall, think back)
- Wondering (ponder, think about, puzzle over, deliberate)
- Imagining (visualize, dream, create)
- Inquiring (question, seek information)
- Interpreting (explain, define)
- Evaluating (assess, estimate, grade)
- Judging (value, size up, rank)

We often use several of these activities in combination to solve a problem or make a decision. We can develop each of these skills individually and then use them in combination to think critically.

Example: We identify or acknowledge a problem, question the possibilities for solving it and analyze each possibility before arriving at a proposed solution.

We observe a problem or situation in the community, wonder what has caused this situation to exist, remember something we read or viewed that was similar and begin to imagine possibilities for a solution.

APPLYING THE ACTIVITIES REQUIRED FOR CRITICAL THINKING

Engage in conversations with your children that require them to apply the thinking activities. This will prepare them to develop critical thinking activities.

When you are talking about a true story or real event, gather factual knowledge to become familiar with the history, principles or context of an issue.

You can do this by being curious, observant, and remembering what you have seen or heard.

Tell your story. Share your experiences and observations with your children. Model for them your ability to think critically.

The following pages provide examples of using the elements of thinking to develop critical thinking skills.

CREATE A SMART BOX/TREASURE CHEST

A wide collection of thoughts to use for creating, imagining, problem solving, and questioning come from ideas that are collected and stored from many different experiences. Observing, information gathering, participating and experiencing are the keys to building a treasure chest full of great thoughts.

Remind children that their collection of facts, ideas, observations and visions become their own SMART BOX/TREASURE CHEST. Apply the suggestions provided to help children to fill their SMART BOX/TREASURE CHEST.

When we are required to solve a problem or come up with a new way of doing something it is important to be able to generate as many solutions as possible. This requires a "treasure chest" of experiences and ideas to choose from. Varied and rich experiences provide children with a full colorful "SMART BOX."

CREATE A SMART BOX/TREASURE CHEST of rich and colorful experiences, ideas and images that can be used to create an array of possible solutions.

This collection of ideas that make up the "SMART BOX" come from every experience and every situation that children participate in or observe.

We can teach them to pay attention to what is going on around them and to ask questions so they can collect facts, ideas, visions even dreams for their "SMART BOX".

We have to be careful not to let good ideas and great teaching/learning opportunities get away. Remind children that every situation presents an opportunity to learn something new and add to our "SMART BOX"/ TREASURE CHEST.

HOW DO WE CREATE THE SMART BOX/TREASURE CHEST?
GATHERING INFORMATION - Building a knowledge base is easier now than ever with access to the internet.

USE CURRENT EVENTS AS A PLATFORM TO CREATE CURIOSITY AND GATHER INFORMATION: Neighborhood events, school events, city events and national events create opportunities for children to ask "What if…" and develop a variety of solutions.

ACTIVITY: Select a current event that is generating a lot of interest.

EXAMPLE: Instruct children to use the computer to access the internet to get additional information on the topic you chose. Have periodic discussions and allow the "expert" to share information with you and the rest of the family.

ACTIVITY: Student is assigned a topic from the newspaper or children's social studies, history or geography textbook. Student is to become the expert on the subject by gathering as much information as possible by going online. Computers are available in the library for this type of research.

LEARN SOMETHING NEW/TRY SOMETHING NEW: Learning something new is one of the best ways to add to the SMART BOX/TREASURE CHEST. Encourage children to try something they haven't done before; learn a new sport, learn to play a musical instrument, learn a foreign language.

STUDENTS –TRY SOMETHING NEW engage in a new activity at school (example: photography club, debate club,). Learning something new and trying something new always presents new information and an opportunity to observe. These are good fillers for the SMART BOX.

PARENTS – LEARN SOMETHING NEW/TRY SOMETHING NEW – Tell your children what you will learn. Select something that really interests you or that you always wanted to do (tennis, golf, salsa dancing, computer classes, yoga, creative writing, cooking classes or a foreign language). Tell your children what you are able to add to your SMART BOX/TREASURE CHEST as a result of your new experiences.

CHANGE THE CHANNEL: Watch the educational science programs with your children and have a contest to see who can collect the most facts for their SMART BOX/TREASURE CHEST. If you are not able to watch the program with your children, direct them to watch the program and then report their new SMART BOX finds or facts to you.

BE OBSERVANT: What did you observe (in the park, on the way home, at the mall, in the classroom, in the cafeteria, at the store) Pay attention to what is going on around you.

THE PARENT SMART BOX/TREASURE CHEST: start your own SMART BOX/ TREAURE CHEST. This will demonstrate to your children that you are continuing to observe and learn. Note your observations, the facts you gather from reading magazines, newspapers, watching news programs, doing on-line research, learning something new.

CREATING YOUR SMART BOX/TREASURE CHEST

PARENTS: Ask children to begin creating their own Smart Box/Treasure Chest.
- **Suggest that they pick a new activity to learn. It can be a sport, dancing, art, or music.**
- **Suggest that they read the newspaper and pick a topic they do not know a lot about and do research on the computer to learn more. The topic may be as different as hurricanes, amusement parks, World cup soccer, the effect of global warming. The important idea here is to learn something new.**
- **Go with your children to a museum you have never visited or have not visited in a long time – talk about what you observe.**

Problem Solving

STEP ONE: Careful Observation

Observe, organize and define the problem or situation.

Observe what is going on around you. Identify the problem or situation. (Careful observation)

Organize and define the problem-Prepare to solve the problem.

ASK THE QUESTIONS: What is the situation now? What would we like the situation to be? That becomes the goal.

What may get in the way of solving the problem? These are the roadblocks.

Ask yourself some questions — What is going on here? What caused this problem? Who needs to be involved in solving this?

STEP TWO: Remembering, Wondering, Inquiring

Think about the problem or situation.

Remember similar situations. - Who solved this problem? What did they do? Why did they do it this way? How did the solution work? How many solutions did they try before finding one that worked?

Wondering — Will any of these solutions work for this problem? Is there more than one problem?

STEP THREE: Inquiring - Learn more about the problem by asking questions so you will understand what you are trying to solve.

Questions – What is the problem? Why is this a problem? What caused this problem? Who needs to be involved in solving this problem? Is there more than one problem? Is there a simple solution to the problem?

STEP FOUR: Imagine and visualize possible solutions - Think outside the box.

Select one of your solutions and think about what you can do to make it the best solution possible.

Evaluate the workability of the proposed solution and make necessary changes.

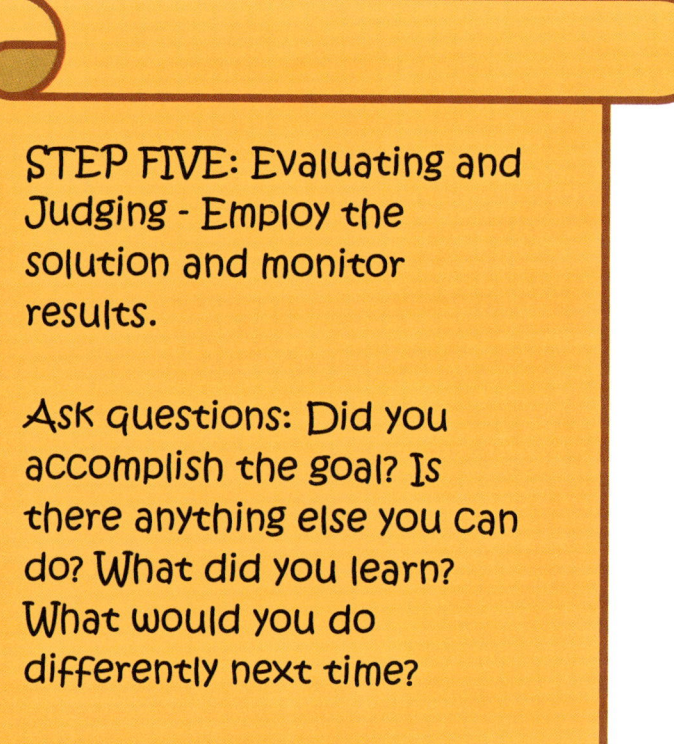

STEP FIVE: Evaluating and Judging - Employ the solution and monitor results.

Ask questions: Did you accomplish the goal? Is there anything else you can do? What did you learn? What would you do differently next time?

Use these questions to think of possible solutions:

What is the problem? Who needs to be involved? Who will help me? What needs to be done? What can I do? Why is this a possible solution? Why do I think this will work?

PROBLEM SOLVING WORKSHEETS

WHAT	
WHO	
WHAT	
WHY	

What is getting in the way?	What can I do about it?

Solutions I Tried...	Results...

THE END RESULT

What happened as a result of the solutions I tried?

_____
_____
_____
_____

TELL YOUR STORY

DON'T MISS AN OPPORTUNITY TO FAN THE FLAMES OF CURIOSITY/TELL YOUR STORY: EXAMPLE: "Nana" came in exhausted but excited after completing her 5th half marathon. She asked her grandson, Miguel "Do you want to see my medal?" He replied with a question "Did you win first place?" Nana explained that everyone who completes a marathon wins a medal. At that point Papa began the explanation of what it means to participate in a marathon and the origin and history of the marathon. Miguel had more facts and images to add to his "SMART BOX".

Children learn by example.

DON'T IGNORE THE POWER OF YOUR EXPERIENCES:
Children love stories. Because you have lived you have some great stories.

TELL STORIES ABOUT: your childhood neighborhood, when you tried out for the soft ball team, your favorite teachers, the classes you hated, the class you had to make up so you would not fail, your challenges on your first job, being on the dean's list, being on the honor roll, your best friend in grammar school, you could go on and on.

All of your experiences give you great material to talk about what you REMEMBER, what you OBSERVED, what you WONDERED about, what you IMAGINED, how you INTERPRETED things going on around you, being CURIOUS, how you EVALUATED and JUDGED situations before you made a decision.

THINKING OUTSIDE THE BOX

IMAGINING POSSIBILITES: This skill also draws from the "treasure chest" The more exposure children have to different ideas and situations the more likely they are to come up with a variety of ideas. What could possibly work here? What could possibly happen here? Consider how others will see the situation (Walk a mile in someone else's moccasins) "What if…?"

REMEMBERING: To effectively use facts and information gathered from observation. Remembering is crucial.
Support children in THINKING OUTSIDE OF THE BOX Encourage your children to:

- ❖ BE OBSERVANT

- ❖ LOOK for situations that could be improved and think of possible improvements

- ❖ OBSERVE when a situation causes them or someone to be dissatisfied or uncomfortable

- ❖ WONDER about the causes for this situation

- ❖ IMAGINE the possibilities for improvement

LET'S GET CURIOUS

CURIOSITY – Get inquisitive – Curiosity will drive the development of varied solutions. What caused this? How did it happen? Has it happened before? Who has been affected? What has been affected? How could it have been prevented? How can we make this better? What if?????

STUDENT ACTIVITY: IT'S ALL ABOUT THE DETAILS - This game requires children to discuss one specific incident or location they observed. They have to state as many details as possible. You can use the basic questions: *What? When? Where?*

EXAMPLE: There was a fire drill today and you could not get your coat. When did this happen? What did you observe? How did people act? What did they do? How did the fire drill affect the rest of the day?

Ask questions that motivate children to be observant of their own actions: How did you act? How did you react to your fellow classmates?

Drawing Conclusions: Based on what you observed, what can you say about the effect of fire drills? If this were a story, what different ending would you write?

> **STUDENT ACTIVITY VARIATIONS**: What did you notice about the people there? How would you describe them? What did they do that causes you to describe them in this way? Use adjectives from your descriptive word list to describe them (cautious, nervous, sad, excited).

Children can compete with one another or you can keep a tally in a notebook for each child and see if they can improve their score by observing more details each time you play.

LOOKING FOR A BETTER WAY: Curiosity takes another form when children can ask "Is there a better way to do this?" If children complain about current processes, systems or procedures suggest that they come up with a "better way."

EXAMPLE: Use a procedure at school that the children don't like. Instruct them to discuss a "better way" to do things.

Possible topics: detention rules, playground rules, recess, cafeteria rules

EXAMPLE: When you take your children to a department store instruct them to walk through and identify procedures that could be improved. Ask how these procedures can be improved and what the benefit will be.

THE QUESTION is: "How can this process, procedure, situation or rule be improved?

WHY, WHY, WHY – Asking "Why?" is one way to get to the cause behind a situation.

WHAT IF??????? EVALUATING OR JUDGING – Evaluate the workability of the proposed solution and make necessary changes.

APPLYING CRITICAL THINKING SKILLS

We get better at any skill when we continue to practice. There are always opportunities to encourage children to apply critical thinking skills.

Repeat the previous activities. Engage in conversations regarding current events, situations that affect them and popular personalities they admire. Encourage children to apply the following skills:

DRAW LOGICAL CONCLUSIONS: Ask children to discuss situations or current events and draw a conclusion based on the facts they have. Ask if they feel the conclusion is logical.

PROVIDE NEW INSIGHT: Encourage children to try a new and imaginative way of looking at a situation, event or problem.

REPRESENT A VARIETY OF PERSPECTIVES: Encourage children to look at situations and issues from other's point of view. EXAMPLE: What do the teachers think about this? How do the neighbors feel about a current neighborhood situation?

SOLVE PROBLEMS WITH EFFECTIVE APPLICATION OF INFORMATION: Encourage children to consider all of the information and resources available for possible solutions to a problem.

PARENTS: Apply these skills to current situations at school, in the neighborhood or current news events.

Talk to children about a recent problem you solved. What was the problem? What information did you use? What was the solution?

PARENTS ARE LEARNING PARTNERS WHEN THEY…
Create an environment at home that encourages children to focus on their academic goals.

- **There is a specific area and a specific time for homework**
- **There are no distractions – NO TV, NO Music, No phone calls, No visitors**

- Instruct children to spend 20-30 minutes correcting mistakes or incorrect answers on previous assignments.
- Direct children to spend time reviewing the assignments in their folder and correcting any mistakes.
- Discuss expectations and establish small goals that lead to a larger goal.

- Encourage children to use the list of descriptive words to describe themselves as they manage their learning challenges.
- Establish dinner conversation as a time to discuss current events and school events (encourage children to ask questions about events, i.e. What caused this? How will this affect others? What if?)
- Create habits (let your children see you doing the things that you ask them to do) i.e. take your children to the library, have your children read to you.
- Encourage children to be curious and ask questions.
- Discuss situations that occur outside of the classroom.

- Remind them to use the strategies you have discussed: bouncing back when things get challenging, breaking a task into small steps, using positive self-talk, asking questions, correcting their mistakes.
- Use the worksheets in this handbook to focus on the strategies discussed (positive self-talk, etc.).

Parents,

As Learning Partners, you realize that you never stop learning. You will emphasize this to your children with your attitude, words and actions.

The activities and strategies that you used in this handbook are presented so you can continue to use them.

Focus on your learning, try different things and share these new experiences and thoughts with your children. You will see as Learning Partners you and your children will continue to grow.

GLOSSARY

Achievement Attitude is a mindset that is focused on improving, getting smarter and getting better. It is a mindset that is not discouraged by setbacks, failure or mistakes.

Achievement Zone representation of the experience children have when they apply Achievement Attitude, Smart Steps and Critical Thinking Skills to learn from their mistakes, bounce back from failure and achieve learning goals.

Bouncing Back continuing to work toward accomplishment of a learning goal despite mistakes or failure.

Critical Thinking Skills
 *skills required to gather, process and use new information effectively to solve problems and generate new ideas.
*skills required to effectively use current knowledge in different ways to generate new ideas and achieve new learning goals.

Learning Partner the parent or other adult who supports children in developing the attitude, habits and critical thinking skills required for continuous learning and achievement.

Smart Box/Treasure Chest a wide collection of thoughts and ideas that are collected from many different experiences and can be used for creating, imagining, problem-solving and questioning.

Smart Steps Specific actions lead to continuous learning and achievement. Learning Partners will teach, model and reinforce these habits to children.

Self-Talk The conversation we have in our head after a success or failure to make sure we don't get discouraged.

Success Factors The thoughts and actions that contribute to the accomplishment of a learning goal.

REFERENCE & RESOURCE GUIDE

Books:

Dweck, Carol S., PhD. *Mindset: The New Psychology of Success*. New York: Random House, 2006.

Dweck, Carol S., PhD. *Self-Theories: Their Role in Motivation, Personality and Development*. Philadelphia: Psychology House Publishers, 2000.

Colvin, Geoff. *Talent is Overrated: What Really Separates World-Class Performers from Everybody Else*. New York: Portfolio, 2008.

Ruggiero, Vincent Ryan. *The Art of Thinking: A Guide to Critical and Creative Thought*. New York: Pearson Longman Publishers, 2007.

Research:

Burnett, Paul C. (2000). "The Impact of Praise on Students' Self-Talk and Self Concepts". Paper presented at annual meeting, American Educational Research Association in Montreal, Quebec, Canada.

Russell, Sue, and Sullivan, Robert. (2000). "Resilience Across Contexts: Family, Work, Culture and Community". Recommendations from a National Invitational Conference.

Hersh C. Waxman, University of Houston
Jon P. Gray, Lamar University
Yolanda N. Padron, University of Houston
(2000)
"Review of Research on Educational Resilience"

Acknowledgements

With deepest gratitude and appreciation I thank everyone who encouraged and supported me as I developed the concept of Parents as Learning Partners into a workshop series and this hand book.

Parents as Learning Partners began as a concept based on my experiences as a Learning and Development Consultant. I observed that there are specific habits that support learning and achievement at every point on the learning continuum. The workshop, train-the-trainer program and the book were developed to support parents in helping their children develop these habits.

I acknowledge this book would not be a finished product without the support, encouragement and actual hard work of wonderful friends and family. Thanks to Kathleen Robbins (my sister), Michael Bennett, Miriam Gonzalzes, Michael Thibodeaux and Paul Cohen for reading my first manuscript and offering feedback and suggestions. Thanks to Roxann Chargois, Rina Campbell and Tony Burroughs for their diligence in reviewing the first edition and providing the feedback (and criticism) that lead to a more user-friendly second edition.

Thanks to all of my family and friends (you know who you are) who encouraged and supported me as I took on this project and learned what it really means to write your first book.

Thanks to my niece, Myriah Weatherspoon, for teaching me how to effectively use my computer to format the book and proving that an adult can learn a lot from a 13 year old.

Thank you to all of the parents who allowed me to use the wonderful photos that added color and expression to the book.

I offer special honor, thanks and appreciation to my parents, the late Clarence and Arvellia Robbins for giving me a great foundation for continuous learning and achievement.

Elaine Robbins Harris

To order additional books go to
www.theinnovativesolutions.com (pay pal available)
or call (773) 779-9942

School districts, Not-for-Profits and Community organizations interested in the workshop or the Train-the-Trainer program that accompanies the *Parents as Learning Partners* handbook, please contact:

Innovative Solutions Consulting
773-779-9942
elaine@theinnovativesolutions.com

Made in the USA
Charleston, SC
11 December 2010